1/14/17

Greg and Cathe Laurie,

Thank you for your faithfulness to the ministry. It's a true honor to sit under your leadership as you diligently teach the word of God. You two are true examples of what it means to follow Christ whole-heartedly while being His hands and feet. Witnessing your godly behavior stirs up a much deeper thirst for the Lord and His word within my own heart and it inspires me to run my race well for our Lord and savior, Jesus Christ. May the Lord continue to pour out His abundant blessings into your marriage and transform you more and more into His image while using you both in a mighty way to bring glory to His name. My prayer is that God will speak directly to you and minister to your hearts as you read through this book. We will all encounter seasons of waiting, but through it all, God will always remain faithful. I pray that whatever season God may have you in, you will wait faithfully on Him, hold fast to Him, and trust Him completely for the road ahead. He will never leave you nor forsake you. Trust Him always and may He bless you abundantly with the richness of His love, grace, and mercy as you seek to honor and keep Him first. Blessings!

1 Cor 15:58

Mac-Lee Mayor

Patiently Waiting on the Lord for a Godly Husband

MAE LEE HAYMON

WESTBOW
PRESS®

A DIVISION OF THOMAS NELSON
& ZONDERVAN

Scripture taken from the New King James Version®. Copyright © 1982 by Thomas Nelson. Used by permission. All rights reserved.

Scripture quotations marked (NLT) are taken from the Holy Bible, New Living Translation, copyright © 1996, 2004, 2007 by Tyndale House Foundation. Used by permission of Tyndale House Publishers, Inc., Carol Stream, Illinois 60188. All rights reserved.

Professional Photography (Author Photo) by Jeff Ellingson

WestBow Press books may be ordered through booksellers or by contacting:

WestBow Press
A Division of Thomas Nelson & Zondervan
1663 Liberty Drive
Bloomington, IN 47403
www.westbowpress.com
1 (866) 928-1240

Because of the dynamic nature of the Internet, any web addresses or links contained in this book may have changed since publication and may no longer be valid. The views expressed in this work are solely those of the author and do not necessarily reflect the views of the publisher, and the publisher hereby disclaims any responsibility for them.

Any people depicted in stock imagery provided by Thinkstock are models, and such images are being used for illustrative purposes only. Certain stock imagery © Thinkstock.

ISBN: 978-1-5127-6396-6 (sc)
ISBN: 978-1-5127-6395-9 (e)

Library of Congress Control Number: 2016918909

Print information available on the last page.

WestBow Press rev. date: 11/28/2016

CONTENTS

DEDICATION

With a joyful heart, this book is dedicated to the many women who desire to have God's best for their lives. If the Lord has promised you a godly husband, my prayer is that you will wait patiently on Him for His blessing to be poured out into your life. God is faithful and He will deliver on all of His promises.

> I, the Lord, have spoken it; it shall come to pass,
> and I will do it; I will not hold back.
> —Ezekiel 24:14a

> So shall My word be that goes forth from My mouth;
> it shall not return to Me void, but it shall accomplish
> what I please, and it shall prosper in
> the thing for which I sent it.
> —Isaiah 55:11

With sweet love and gratitude, this book is also dedicated to my future godly husband:

You are my own priceless and precious gift from the Lord. I thank God for you everyday. I'm looking forward to that God-appointed time when we will finally meet and rejoice in Him for bringing us together. Until then, I will continue to wait patiently and expectantly on the Lord for you. I love you!

> Every good gift and every perfect gift is from above,
> and comes down from the Father of lights.
> —James 1:17a

INTRODUCTION

Over the past eight years, I have been praying and asking the Lord to bless me with a godly husband. During the first three to four years of praying, I took it upon myself and made a list of the different qualities I desired in a future mate (things I wanted and things I didn't want). These character traits were all written down in a prayer journal, and over time, additions and revisions were made. My journaling for the perfect godly husband lasted for three full years. Finally, the realization that I was not consulting God and entrusting my list to Him dawned on me. In essence, these were the desires of my own heart. Well, the Lord quickly showed me that there is no such thing as a perfect godly spouse and that I needed to relinquish my list to Him. He was leading and directing me to begin praying in the Spirit and according to His perfect will for His divine choice in a godly husband. To say the least, it was very challenging to intercede in this way, based on my lack of trust in God and immature thinking at the time. With certainty, I thought I knew what was best for me. Needless to say, the Lord gave me a wake-up call and made it very clear that I don't know everything and that His ways are higher than my ways—as well as His thoughts than my thoughts (Isaiah 55:9b).

After this realization, my prayers radically changed as I began interceding for God's choice in a godly husband. Years of fervent prayer and godly encouragement from the body of Christ, along with God's confirmation, have given me hope to rest and wait patiently on the Lord for His best choice in a godly husband of promise. My future mate has already been preselected, pre-appointed, and predestined by God before the foundations of the world, and He desires to write our love story.

As you read through this book, my prayer is that you will be encouraged and richly blessed as you wait on God's best! I encourage you to stay committed to the Lord in waiting on Him for your own godly husband. If He has made this promise to you, believe and trust in Him that He Himself will be faithful in bringing it to pass. Allow the Lord to write your love story.

For all the promises of God in Him are Yes, and in
Him Amen, to the glory of God through us.
—2 Corinthians 1:20

God is your Husband first. Listening to biblical messages and sermons, I've heard it said time and time again that no man can meet all of your needs. Only Jesus can, and He will be faithful to do so. He understands and knows you better than you know yourself. The psalmist says in Psalm 139:1–4,

O Lord, You have searched me and known me. You know my sitting down and my rising up; You understand my thought afar off. You comprehend my path and my lying down, and are acquainted with all my ways. For there is not a word on my tongue, but behold, O Lord, You know it altogether.

Please keep Jesus as your first love. He will be your faithful Husband, Counselor, Provider, Protector, Friend, Defender, as well as the Lover of your soul, and His love for you will far exceed any human love. When the Lord brings you your godly husband here on this earth, do not put this man on some pedestal or idolize him in any shape or form. If you do, you will be very disappointed. Understandably, your godly husband is a wonderful gift and blessing from the Lord, but you do not want to turn him into an idol. Exodus 20:3–5a exhorts us by affirming,

You shall have no other gods before Me. You shall not make for yourself a carved image-any likeness of anything that is in heaven above, or that is in the earth beneath, or that is in the water under the earth; you shall not bow down to them nor serve them. For I, the Lord your God, am a jealous God.

I highly encourage you to keep God first, not just in your love life, but also in all areas of your life. He needs and should be everything to you. He is faithful to meet all of your needs. Jesus told the Samaritan woman who had five husbands in John 4:14,

But whoever drinks of the water that I shall give him will never thirst. But the water that I shall give him will become in him a fountain of water springing up into everlasting life.

Run to the fountain of God's living waters and freely drink from it. Don't put pressure on your future husband by expecting him to meet all of your needs. Remember he is human just like you, and he's incapable of fulfilling what only Jesus can do. Instead, have a thirst for the Lord who is more than able to give you everything you need and more. John 7:37b says, "If anyone thirsts, let him come to Me and drink." The Lord loves you with an everlasting love, and His desire is for you to keep Him first and run to Him with all your cares and concerns. He is your Savior, and He will never disappoint you.

Patiently Waiting on the Lord for a Godly Husband originated from my life experiences and the lessons I've learned, and I'm still learning along the way as I patiently wait on the Lord to bring forth His promise in my life. As you read through the pages of this book, my prayer is that your heart will be strengthened and your hope renewed as you get a firsthand look at how the Lord can work, teach, and show you in your own personal journey to wait patiently on Him for your godly husband of promise.

CHAPTER 1

WAITING ON GOD'S BEST

WAITING CAN BE A real challenge for anyone. How many of us enjoy waiting? We live in a society where waiting is an inconvenience and certainly doesn't fit into our daily schedules. Living in Los Angeles, it seems all I do is wait and wait. It can be waiting to be seated at a restaurant, waiting in line to see a movie, waiting to be helped at a department store, or waiting in traffic. It can be nerve-racking and tiresome. However, the Bible admonishes believers to wait on the Lord, and their hearts will be strengthened by Him as they do (Psalm 27:14). His desire is for us to exercise patience while waiting on Him to bring us our own godly husbands of promise. James 1:4 says, "But let patience have its perfect work, that you may be perfect and complete, lacking nothing."

Praying for the Lord's choice in a godly husband will involve waiting on Him to bring this promise to pass. It will require you to patiently wait on His timing and not your own.

> He has made everything beautiful in its time.
> —Ecclesiastes 3:11a

In my earlier years of praying for a godly husband, I believed that once I prayed, the answer would come to pass instantaneously.

Needless to say, it didn't happen in that sense. A whole year went by and I found myself deeply discouraged. After having a pity party for several days, my thoughts were to fast and pray, and then the Lord would surely answer and bring me my godly Prince Charming. And we would court for a year, have a beautiful wedding, and then ride off into the sunset by a horse-drawn carriage and live happily ever after. Instead, my plans went south again and I turned up empty-handed.

At this point, the questions were raised as to why my prayers were not being answered. Continuing in prayer, the Lord began to reveal to me that although prayer and fasting are important spiritual aspects and should be incorporated into every believer's life, I couldn't force His hand into making something happen when it wasn't His timing yet. We need to realize that there is nothing you or I can do in our own capabilities to bring about the promises of God.

Think about the story of Abraham and Sarah. The Lord had promised them a son, and during their twenty-five-year waiting period, it seemed as though the promise of a child was farfetched, causing them to grow anxious. The couple tried in their own strength to bring about the promised son through their maid, Hagar, which resulted in heartache, distress, and grief. This was definitely not part of God's plan.

My scenario is different, but I can relate to their anxiousness and weariness in waiting as I tried to bring about the Lord's promise of a godly husband through online dating. My thought process at the time was that I needed to help God out by signing up for Internet dating services. In my mind, this was the only solution to my ongoing prayer. But even before signing up, the Lord spoke to me through His Word as well as other believers and gave me a resounding "No!"

Needless to say, I didn't listen to God and signed up anyway, thinking this was the best plan. The Lord made it very clear that He always knows best and my thought process was fickle, to say the least. Although I was disobedient, He still placed His hedge of protection around me. During the three-month course of my online dating experience, 98 percent of the guys who showed an interest or vice versa didn't live in the state of California. They were all back East. God knew I had no interest in a long-distance relationship. It was His way of reiterating the no that He had said to begin with. He's saying no now, and the answer will always be no. You would think that this would make me take down my profile, but I thought otherwise. Eventually I met people who were geographically desirable, but there were red flags in the process. They were nice guys, but the Lord's answer remained firm and He closed the doors immediately. As a result, I took down my profile and asked the Lord to forgive me for my willful disobedience. Looking back on that experience gave me revelation on how my faith and trust in the Lord was severely lacking, as well as my unbelief in His sovereignty of bringing me His best choice in a godly husband.

Ladies, never run or walk ahead of the Lord in any given situation. You will only make things worse for yourself and create more problems. Please realize there is nothing you can do in your own strength to bring about the promises of God. He doesn't need our help. Don't be foolish as I was and think that you can undermine God's authority and win. You will lose every time.

> The Lord knows people's thoughts; he
> knows they are worthless.
> —Psalm 94:11 (NLT)

Going back to the story of Abraham and Sarah, I loved how the Lord redeemed them in spite of their shortcomings. He remained faithful to His Word in giving the couple Isaac, the son He had promised to them.

> If we are faithless, He remains faithful;
> He cannot deny Himself.
> —2 Timothy 2:13

Our Lord is faithful and will do the same for you and me as we patiently wait on His timing and His choice for a godly husband of promise. The psalmist says in Psalm 40:1, "I waited patiently for the Lord; and He inclined to me, and heard my cry." The godly woman realizes that the promised husband is worth the wait. During this time of waiting, the Lord is molding, equipping, and shaping her to be the godly wife He has called her to be for her husband of promise. If God has spoken to you and confirmed you will be someone's wife, consider this a high calling that shouldn't be taken for granted. Therefore, wait on the Lord. He loves you very much, and He wants to give you His very best.

> Wait on the Lord; be of good courage, and He shall
> strengthen your heart; Wait, I say, on the Lord!
> —Psalm 27:14

> Every good gift and every perfect gift is from above,
> and comes down from the Father of lights, with
> whom there is no variation or shadow of turning.
> —James 1:17

CHAPTER 2

HOW DO YOU KNOW IF
THE LORD HAS PROMISED
YOU A HUSBAND?

AS WOMEN, OUR NEEDS and desires differ on a variety of scales. These factors might include a need for physical and emotional healing, deliverance from an addiction, guidance in a certain situation, direction in life, the love of family and friends to having or maintaining a job, financial help, shelter, and other important life provisions. On the other hand, women in general have their own personal wants. Some may desire to have a designer handbag, the luxury of a new car every three years, a new outfit every month, the joy of vacationing in some exquisite place each year, and/or the desire to have a godly husband.

Some of the things listed above contain needs and desires I've longed and prayed for in my own personal life. There have been times when I've asked God to heal me from emotional distress, to impart His wisdom in difficult circumstances, for guidance, and for financial assistance. Aside from my needs, my greatest desire is to have a godly husband who will love me as Christ loves the church. Constant prayer has been lifted up on my behalf from my sisters in Christ for God to give me His very best. In my own time of intercessory prayer, the Lord has shown me through His

Word that my greatest need and desire should always be for Him first and foremost. Everyone and everything else should pale in comparison. Deuteronomy 6:5 and Exodus 20:3–5 are two important verses the Lord has laid on my heart that have been incorporated into my daily prayers. Loose paraphrase: I shall love the Lord with all of my heart, soul, and strength. I must not bow down or worship any idols, for the Lord my God is a Jealous God who will not tolerate my affection for any other gods. What I believe the Lord is saying is He should always come first in my life, and my love for Him should far exceed the love of any other person or thing.

There was a pivotal time in my life when I distinctly remember praying to God with heartfelt tears and asking if it was in His divine plan for me to remain single. If it was indeed the case, my request then was for the Lord to remove the desire for a godly mate out of my heart completely and for Him to continue to strengthen me to serve Him and do His will regardless of my marital status. This was a very difficult prayer, but in the midst of my grief, I felt prompted by the Holy Spirit to do so. Even though my desire is to be married some day, I didn't want to spend the rest of my life praying for this dream if it wasn't in God's plans. After months of fervent prayer, the Lord answered my request by revealing it through scripture that He wants me to wait patiently on Him for His best choice in a godly husband. Additional confirmation came through word of mouth by other believers who were essentially saying the same thing, "Wait on the Lord for a godly husband."

Ladies, your greatest need is Christ Himself. He is your Husband, and His love for you runs deeper than what any man can give you. He cares about all of your needs, desires, and the deepest longings of your hearts. By no means am I saying that if you pray for any and everything that the Lord will just grant you your request. God will meet all of your needs, and He will answer all your prayer requests according to His perfect will for your life. If you desire anyone or anything above the Lord, or place a higher priority on having those things above your relationship with Christ, you have fallen into the sin of idolatry. Remember, ladies, the Lord should always be first in every area of your life. No one and nothing should take the place that rightly belongs to God Himself. The Lord will be faithful to answer your prayers, and His answer will either be yes, no, or wait. We need to learn to be content with whatever answer He gives and realize that He knows what's best for our lives. I encourage you all to spend quality time in His Word while praying and asking Him if He has indeed promised you a husband. God primarily speaks through His Word. While you are seeking the Lord for an answer, ask Him to prepare your heart for His response. Keep in mind that God always has your best interest at heart. His plans for you are for good and not for disaster to give you a future and a hope (Jeremiah 29:11 NLT).

Our Lord is faithful, and whether His answer is yes, no, or wait, He will give you His grace and the strength to endure and accept His perfect will for your life.

If His divine plan includes a godly husband, wait patiently and expectantly on Him as He prepares you and your husband for each other. Wait on His perfect timing. Pray and ask the Lord for His divine choice in a godly man—one who is Spirit filled, one who is walking in the Spirit, and not fulfilling the lusts of the flesh. Additionally, pray and ask the Lord to bless you with a godly man who will love Jesus more than he loves you, someone who will love you as Christ loves the church, a godly man of integrity, a godly man who will stand up for the truth of God's Word and not compromise his faith, a godly man who will honor you as the woman he is courting, a godly man who will honor you as his godly wife and best friend, a godly man who will honor, respect, and fight for his marriage, a godly man who will only have eyes for you and not other women, and a godly man whose talk matches his walk. With men this is impossible, but with God all things are possible (Matthew 19:26b). God has His very best for you!

> And my God shall supply all your need according
> to His riches in glory by Christ Jesus.
> —Philippians 4:19

> Be anxious for nothing, but in everything by
> prayer and supplication, with thanksgiving, let your
> requests be made known to God; and the peace of
> God, which surpasses all understanding, will guard
> your hearts and minds through Christ Jesus.
> —Philippians 4:6–7

> I do not seek My own will but the will
> of the Father who sent Me.
> —John 5:30b

> No good thing will He withhold from
> those who walk uprightly.
> —Psalm 84:11b

CHAPTER 3

LEARNING TO LOVE
THE LORD FIRST

IN THIS TIME OF waiting on the Lord for my godly husband of promise, there have been occasions when I've met people who I thought were possibly God's chosen for me. I distinctly remember in each situation I would ask the Lord questions, such as "Is this the one?" "Is this my Prince Charming?" or "Is this my future godly husband?" My questions were followed by thoughts of where our first date would be, how long we would court, when we would get married, and where we would honeymoon.

My mind would always kick into overdrive when meeting someone. I was determined to get this ball rolling so I could start planning my wedding. In those moments, my thoughts would be consumed with that particular individual at the time. I found myself double-checking my phone to see if he had texted me or not. And when I didn't receive a text, I would become discouraged and begin analyzing the situation. Did I say the wrong words? Did I do something to scare him away? To say the least, the Lord intervened and stopped this high-speed thought process I was entertaining in my mind.

The Lord gently and lovingly showed me through His Word that I was on the borderline of idol worship and I was placing the desire to have a man above Him. He also affirmed to me that I needed to live out Deuteronomy 6:5: "You shall love the Lord your God with all your heart, with all your soul, and with all your strength." In other words, Jesus needs to be my first love and number 1 priority in all areas of my life. I need to love the Lord more than my future godly husband of promise and diligently keep Jesus at the very center of my life.

Learning to incorporate Deuteronomy 6:5 into my daily life was a real challenge. Don't get me wrong. I do love the Lord. Matthew 26:41b says, "The spirit indeed is willing, but the flesh is weak." My flesh didn't want me to apply this spiritual truth to my daily walk. I knew it was the enemy whispering in my ear that I didn't have to do this. Knowing this fact gave me more of a reason to run to God and ask Him to graciously give me His strength and the perseverance to love Him with all of my heart, soul, and strength. The Lord is so faithful! After praying this verse for a month and a half, the Lord led me to write down this scripture on three-by-five cards and put it up in my cubicle at work, in my car, and all over my house so it will be ingrained in my mind and thoughts.

Ladies, the Lord wants us to learn how to love Him first and foremost more than our godly husbands of promise, and what better way than to start now before the Lord brings him to you? We have to remember that the Lord wants our whole heart, not a divided one. Pray and begin asking the Lord to give you His wisdom on how to love Him more than your future husband. Ask Him to give you a desire to do so. Keep in mind the Lord doesn't want us obsessing or idolizing our godly husbands of promise.

Below are essential truths the Lord has placed on my heart about what it means to love and honor Him as my Savior, followed up with waiting on Him for my godly husband of promise. I would like to encourage you with these principles.

LOVE AND KEEP HIM FIRST

Love the Lord above all else, and always keep Him as your first love. The Lord is your Heavenly Husband, and He commands you to love Him with all of your heart, soul, and strength. As your Bridegroom, He will be faithfully devoted to you while deeply loving you, caring for you, continuously forgiving you, and cherishing you now and for all eternity. He will always hold you in His everlasting arms and affirm His love to you over and over again. He will never leave nor forsake you. When you are sad, He will be there to wipe away your tears and comfort your hurting heart.

As your Heavenly Husband, He will always carry you through all seasons of life. He will be your strong support system and number 1 encourager. Love the Lord as your first love, and believe and know that He is the only One who can give you full and complete satisfaction your soul deeply longs for. His love for you is everlasting! As your faithful Bridegroom, He desires for you to be His faithful, godly, and devoted wife in full submission to Him, loving Him above everyone and everything else including your godly husband of promise. As His bride, diligently love, submit, obey, and reverence the Lord, your God, at all times.

For your Maker is your husband, the Lord of hosts
is His name; and your Redeemer is the Holy One of
Israel; He is called the God of the whole earth.
—Isaiah 54:5

Jesus said to him, "You shall love the Lord your God with
all your heart, with all your soul, and with all your mind."
—Matthew 22:37

But seek first the kingdom of God and His righteousness,
and all these things shall be added to you.
—Matthew 6:33

SEEK TO PLEASE THE LORD AND NOT OTHERS

Remember, ladies, you belong to the Lord, and He comes first in every single area of your life. Pray fervently and ask God to give you a heart's desire to please Him first and foremost. Make His plans your plans, His desires your desires, His wants your wants, and His choices your choices. Seek the Lord for His wisdom on how to live a life that is pleasing to Him, regardless of what other people may say or think and what the world's culture says to be true. Live faithfully for Him and not for yourself or anyone else seeking to please the Lord in everything you say and do.

There's no way you can live a sinless or perfect life, but you can pray and ask God to help you live in a way that brings glory and honor to His name. One day you will stand before God and give an account for the way you have lived. The Lord will also reward you for your faithfulness in living for Him and seeking to please Him in all that you have said and done.

> For do I now persuade men, or God? Or do I
> seek to please men? For if I still pleased men, I
> would not be a bondservant of Christ.
> —Galatians 1:10

> Therefore we make it our aim, whether present
> or absent, to be well pleasing to Him.
> —2 Corinthians 5:9

> And whatever you do, do it heartily, as to the Lord
> and not to men, knowing that from the Lord you will
> receive the reward of the inheritance;
> for you serve the Lord Christ.
> —Colossians 3:23–24

So then each of us shall give account of himself to God.
—Romans 14:12

SPENDING QUALITY TIME WITH THE LORD

This biblical principle along with the other ones listed above and below does not stop when He brings you your godly husband of promise. They are ongoing and continual fundamental truths. It's important for you to maintain and cultivate your personal relationship with the Lord. Ladies, you need Him every second, every moment, and in every season of your life. God's Word is infused with His wisdom, attributes, love, guidance, blessings, commands, direction, discernment, life instructions, and much more. You need to hear from the Lord on what He has to say to you as you make everyday decisions and life choices. You don't want to lean on your own understanding or allow your emotions to lead you. Doing so will cause you to go down the wrong path.

Not only do you need God's wisdom in your day-to-day life, you will also need it in your future marriage (e.g., how to be the godly wife that the Lord is calling you to be, how to encourage and pray for your husband, how to love and forgive him, and in those times when you have marital issues). Remember that no marriage is perfect. Please don't neglect your time in God's Word or prayer. It's absolutely necessary and shouldn't be taken for granted. Jesus spent time with His Father; therefore, we should follow His example. Daily communion with the Lord is a vital factor in your walk with Him. The more time you spend with Him, the more you will grow into a deeper relationship with the Lord and be transformed into the image of Christ.

This Book of the Law shall not depart from
your mouth, but you shall meditate in it day and night,

that you may observe to do according
to all that is written in it.
—Joshua 1:8a

Get wisdom! Get understanding! Do not forget, nor turn
away from the words of my mouth. Do not forsake her, and
she will preserve you; love her, and she will keep you.
—Proverbs 4:5–6

Now in the morning, having risen a long while
before daylight, He went out and departed to
a solitary place; and there He prayed.
—Mark 1:35

But the wisdom that is from above is first pure,
then peaceable, gentle, willing to yield, full of mercy and
good fruits, without partiality and without hypocrisy.
—James 3:17

OBEY THE LORD ALWAYS AND KEEP HIM AS YOUR PRIMARY FOCUS

Remain obedient to the Lord in everything, regardless of your circumstances. Life is filled with ups and downs, twists and turns, and bumps along the road. Hardships and trials will come your way unexpectedly. It's inevitable! In those moments, you can either allow fear to creep in and cloud your judgment, or you can turn to God, trust in Him, and allow Him to lead you in the way you should go. The Bible tells us in John 16:33, "In the world you will have tribulation; but be of good cheer, I (referring to Jesus) have overcome the world."

Even though you face difficulties, you don't have to be afraid. Instead, be encouraged that the Lord is with you, and He will be faithful to walk you through those challenging times. Your trials are not in vain. They are to correct, protect, or teach you life lessons that you may not otherwise learn apart from the storms of life. The testings of your faith will turn out for God's glory and for your ultimate good. It's always important to trust in and obey the Lord in everything while continuously seeking Him for His wisdom, guidance, and direction on a daily basis, especially during life's darkest seasons. You need Him to lead you down the right path. Please don't lean on your own understanding, because it will cause you to deviate from the direction He wants you to walk in. Instead, keep the Lord close to your heart and as your primary focus. Be sensitive to His Holy Spirit and follow His lead. He may ask you to do something that doesn't seem logical, but obey Him anyway. He is the Spirit of Truth.

The Bible declares in John 16:13–14,

> However, when He, the Spirit of Truth, has come, He will guide you into all truth; for He will not speak on His own authority, but whatever He hears He will speak; and He will tell you things to come. He will glorify Me, for He will take of what is Mine and declare it to you.

The Lord knows exactly what He's doing. Every one of our trials has a higher purpose being fulfilled than what we are able to see in the moment. It will be revealed in time either this side of heaven or when we go home to be with the Lord. All our trials will bring glory to God and will be for our good as they strengthen our faith in Him. Remain obedient to the Lord, and keep Him as your number 1 focus. Adhering to God's Word will deepen your trust and faith in Him while bringing peace to your soul, heart, and mind. The Lord desires for you to live your life in full obedience to Him. You will face ridicule and rejection for abiding by God's standards, but in the end, your faithful obedience will be followed by His awe-inspiring blessings.

> But this is what I commanded them, saying,
> "Obey My voice, and I will be your God, and you shall
> be My people. And walk in all the ways that I have
> commanded you, that it may be well with you."
> —Jeremiah 7:23

> He is the Rock, His work is perfect; for all His
> ways are justice, a God of truth and without
> injustice; Righteous and upright is He.
> —Deuteronomy 32:4

> Trust in the Lord with all your heart, and lean
> not on your own understanding; in all your ways
> acknowledge Him, and He shall direct your paths.
> —Proverbs 3:5–6

> And we know that all things work together
> for good to those who love God, to those who
> are the called according to His purpose.
> —Romans 8:28

FOCUSING SOLELY ON GOD

Social media, entertainment, recreational activities, and sports, among other things, have become integral parts of many cultures around the world. There is nothing wrong with these elements, as they were created for our enjoyment. However, if they are not kept in their proper context, they can become a tool in the enemy's hand in order to draw our attention away from the Lord. Our primary focus should be on the Lord Himself. Everyone and everything else is secondary.

God desires to have close fellowship with us on a daily basis. Your relationship with the Lord should be at the top of the list for most important things. He comes first, and you need Him in every aspect of your life. Situations will arise and storms will come in your life. If the Lord is not your number 1 priority, it will cause you to seek guidance, direction, and wisdom from a source other than the Lord when hardships or problems come your way. Instead, discipline yourself and make God your primary focus so when challenges occur, you will be more inclined to run to and lean on Him. He will sustain you and give you His peace during those difficult seasons. The Lord will be your Guide, your Anchor, and the Rock you can lean on in times of adversity. He is and will always remain faithful! Keep Jesus as your main focus.

> You will keep him in perfect peace, whose mind
> is stayed on You, because he trusts in You.
> —Isaiah 26:3

> Let this mind be in you which was also in Christ Jesus.
> —Philippians 2:5

ACCEPTING HIS WILL VERSUS YOUR OWN WILL

The Lord always has your best interest at heart and desires to reveal His will to you as you diligently seek Him. His plans for you are for your good and for His glory. Your Savior knows you better than you know yourself. He understands you; He knows what you can handle and what you can't; He knows your likes and dislikes; He knows what you think before the thought even enters your mind; He knows what will happen in your life before it takes place; He knows you inside and out; and He knows all things. As your loving Creator, He already has foreknowledge of the plans He has for you. They are exceedingly better than your aspirations, goals, and ambitions. Pray and ask God to help you lay down and permanently abandon your will. Instead, lovingly embrace and accept His perfect will for your life. God's adventure and journey for your life is far more enriching, exciting, and mind-blowing than anything you can achieve on your own. God has and will always have your very best interest at heart.

> For I know the thoughts that I think toward
> you, says the Lord, thoughts of peace and not
> of evil, to give you a future and a hope.
> —Jeremiah 29:11

> Teach me to do Your will, for You are my God; Your
> Spirit is good. Lead me in the land of uprightness.
> —Psalm 143:10

> I have come that they may have life, and that
> they may have it more abundantly.
> —John 10:10b

PATIENTLY AND EXPECTANTLY WAIT ON THE LORD TO BRING YOU HIS BEST CHOICE

Please don't move ahead of the Lord by trying to bring about the promise on your own. When you do, things get messy, and not only do you hurt yourself but others too as they are affected by your actions. Patience is a virtue; wait on the Lord. Isaiah 64:4b says that God acts for the one who waits for Him. Wait patiently on the Lord. Trust that He is working on your behalf and orchestrating your steps and the steps of your godly husband in order for you both to meet. Allow the Lord to do His work, graciously and politely keep your hands out of it, and trust Him to bring the promise to pass. God wants to be the Author of your love story.

The Lord is good to those who wait for
Him, to the soul who seeks Him.
—Lamentations 3:25

I, the Lord, have spoken it; it shall come
to pass, and I will do it.
—Ezekiel 24:14a

HAPPILY ACCEPTING THE GODLY HUSBAND THAT GOD HAS ORDAINED FOR YOU

We all have an idea of the man we desire to marry. Several years ago when I began praying for a godly husband, I made up a list of qualities I desired in a spouse. Over a period of time, the Lord began showing me through His Word to trust Him wholeheartedly in His plan for a godly husband of promise. He has someone in mind far better than my list of quality traits. My checklist was good, but the Lord's choice is one thousand times better because it will bring glory, honor, and praise to His holy name. The Lord never fails when He blesses you. He will always give you His very best! Happily accept His divine choice in a godly mate. There is no such thing as the perfect husband, but God has already hand-selected a first-class mate just for you. He makes no mistakes. Just as you and I have flaws, our future husbands will have imperfections too. But with the Lord in the center of our godly friendships, courtships, and marriages, He will definitely use our strengths and weaknesses so we can help encourage and build each other up in Him for His glory.

Furthermore, we cannot allow our husbands to become idols in our lives and take the place of God. Exodus 20:3 says, "You shall have no other gods before Me." Loose paraphrase: we shall not put our husbands, children, relationships, other people, our careers, material possessions, hobbies, ministries, and you name it before the Lord. Yes, our husbands are gifts from the Lord, but we must keep things in perspective; the Lord is our first love. He is our priority, then our husbands, others, and finally ourselves. We are all familiar with the meaning of this acronym: JOY (Jesus, others, yourself). If you incorporate these truths into your daily walk, you will grow into a deeper relationship with the Lord and experience Him in ways you never have before.

> Then Mary said, "Behold the maidservant of the Lord! Let it be to me according to your word." And the angel departed from her.
> —Luke 1:38

> So then, they are no longer two but one flesh. Therefore what God has joined together, let not man separate.
> —Matthew 19:6

> As it is written: There is none righteous, no, not one.
> —Romans 3:10

> Two are better than one, because they have a good reward for their labor.
> —Ecclesiastes 4:9

HONORING AND RESPECTING YOUR HUSBAND AS UNTO THE LORD

Ladies, God has called us to honor and respect our husbands as to the Lord. We must do so with love, gentleness, and self-control. Honor him by speaking well of him in public and behind closed doors, diligently encourage him with the Word of God, fervently pray for him, and appropriately place his needs before your own.

Respect your husband, and be faithful in obeying him. The husband is the head of the wife. However, if your husband is asking you to do something that contradicts scripture, such as lie, cheat on your taxes, or engage in some form of immoral or illegal activity, you are under no obligation to obey him. Additionally, if your husband is physically abusive to you or your children or if you are in danger, please contact your local authorities right away. Your safety and the safety of your children are very important. In these cases, your obedience to God's standards will overrule obedience to your husband. God will not hold you accountable for objecting to your husband's abuse. Also reach out to your church community for support and biblical counseling.

Ladies, it's very important for us to be praying for our husbands and their spiritual leadership inside and outside the home on a daily basis. The enemy is hard at work and will do and use anything to destroy our marriages. Pray and be watchful! As future wives, God wants us to honor and respect our husbands; however, He wants us to do so in a way that is well pleasing to Him.

> Let the wife see that she respects her husband.
> —Ephesians 5:33b

> But the midwives feared God, and did not do as the king of Egypt commanded them, but saved the male children alive.
> —Exodus 1:17

BE A SUBMISSIVE AND PRAYING WIFE

The word *submissive* can be a controversial term. *The Noah Webster's 1828 American Dictionary of the English Language* defines submission as "humble or supplicant behavior," "the act of yielding to power or authority," and "surrender of the person and power to the control or government of another." Some people cringe when they hear this word. It's human nature to rebel instead of submit. There have been times in my life where I've had a rebellious attitude and did the very opposite of what I was told to do. The fact of the matter is that we are all submissive to those in authority over us, whether it's our boss at work, law enforcement (e.g., obeying the law), government agencies (e.g., paying your taxes), or the leadership of an organization. We are called to submit or we will face the consequences for not doing so.

In the same sense, God calls us to be submissive wives to our husbands. This doesn't mean that you are of less value or less important than your husband; God views you both as equals. However, He has established order in the home with the husband being head of the wife as Christ is head of the church. As a wife, you are to fulfill your role by being submissive to your husband as unto the Lord. Ask the Lord to give you His strength, wisdom, grace, love, and guidance to live this out. In Paul's letter to the Ephesians (5:22), he said, "Wives, submit to your own husbands, as to the Lord." In Philippians 1:6, Paul exhorts the church at Philippi by saying, "Being confident of this very thing, that He who has begun a good work in you will complete it until the day of Jesus Christ."

Ladies, submit to your own husbands as unto the Lord. These are our marching orders from God Himself. Do not do it for your husband. Let's be honest. If you are being submissive for him, you would only do it when you feel like he deserves it. This is the reason scripture says, "Submit to them as unto the Lord." In other words, submit to him whether you feel like it or not, submit to him when he is unlovable (and yes, there will be those times), and most importantly, submit to him because the Lord has called you to be an obedient wife. On that final day, you will give an account to God for not just being a submissive wife but for the life you have lived.

Don't undermine your husband's authority. This can be challenging at times, but remember your heavenly Father is watching, and He will reward you for your faithfulness. Now I must say this: Under no circumstances are you to submit to your husband if he is asking or telling you to do something sinful or contrary to God's Word. In these circumstances, pray for the Lord to open up your husband's eyes to the truth of His Word, and if need be, contact the pastoral staff or a ministry leader at your church for biblical guidance and/or counseling.

Along with submission, be diligent in praying for your husband daily. Pray and ask God to mold him into the godly husband that the Lord desires him to be. Pray for him to be a godly father and for his spiritual leadership. Pray that he will always reflect the heart of Jesus to those around him, pray for his job so his work performance will always bring glory to God, and pray for him to be a shining light to his peers as well as to his management team. Pray for him to always take a stand for Jesus and not compromise his faith. Pray he would have a heart of integrity and be honest in all his ways. In addition, pray for his health and for God's hedge of protection around him. Pray that your husband will always be a faithful and wise steward over all his financial affairs. Overall, pray for your husband fervently, passionately, consistently, and without ceasing.

> Wives, submit to your own husbands, as to the Lord.
> For the husband is head of the wife, as also Christ is
> head of the church; and He is the Savior of the body.
> Therefore, just as the church is subject to Christ, so let
> the wives be to their own husbands in everything.
> —Ephesians 5:22–24

There is neither Jew nor Greek, there is neither
slave nor free, there is neither male nor female;
for you are all one in Christ Jesus.
—Galatians 3:28

Praying always with all prayer and supplication
in the Spirit, being watchful to this end with all
perseverance and supplication for all the saints.
—Ephesians 6:18

LOVE AND FORGIVE YOUR HUSBAND, WHETHER YOU FEEL LIKE IT OR NOT

There will be times when your husband disappoints you and
seems unlovable, but as a woman of God, you are called to forgive
and love your husband as unto the Lord. Keep God as your main
focus and do it unto Him and not your husband. The Lord loves
you so much that He went to the cross on your behalf and died for
your sins in order that you may have eternal life. He is risen and
His love for you runs deeper than any ocean; it's an everlasting
love. With His unending love, Christ Jesus offers forgiveness to
anyone who asks Him. The Bible says, "If we confess our sins,
He is faithful and just to forgive us our sins and to cleanse us
from all unrighteousness" (1 John 1:9). Jesus is a forgiving God;
therefore, imitate Christ in loving and forgiving your husband as
unto the Lord.

Therefore be imitators of God as dear children.
And walk in love, as Christ also has loved us and
given Himself for us, an offering and a sacrifice
to God for a sweet-smelling aroma.
—Ephesians 5:1–2

This is My commandment, that you love
one another as I have loved you.
—John 15:12

Love suffers long and is kind; love does not envy; love does
not parade itself, is not puffed up; does not behave rudely,
does not seek its own, is not provoked, thinks no evil; does not
rejoice in iniquity, but rejoices in the truth; bears all things,
believes all things, hopes all things, endures all things.
—1 Corinthians 13:4–7

And be kind to one another, tenderhearted, forgiving
one another, even as God in Christ forgave you.
—Ephesians 4:32

These things may seem burdensome, but in essence, they are
blessings, and each of us will be rewarded by the Lord for applying
these timeless truths to our everyday lives. Maybe some of you
struggle with the above list. I know I have, especially with the last
one: loving my husband when he is unlovable. I find it easier to
pray for the Lord to rebuke him instead. But that's not the Lord's
heart. His desire is for you and me to love our husbands through
His eyes. Our God is faithful and mighty and He will show you
how to do so through His enabling and strength while molding
and shaping you into the godly wife He has called you to be.

CHAPTER **4**

RESTING IN THE LORD

RESTING IS A VERY important aspect of my life. I enjoy sleeping in when I have the opportunity. My schedule is pretty busy, so I make sure to set ample time aside to get some R&R. According to a Gallup poll, 59 percent of Americans get seven or more hours of sleep at night while the other 41 percent get less than seven hours. From this study, it's safe to say that rest is vital and highly needed to function in our daily lives.

As godly women walking with the Lord, He requires us to rest in Him. There will be seasons in our lives where this can pose as a real challenge. It is in those hard times that we really need to be on our faces before the Lord, asking Him for His peace, wisdom, and strength while resting in Him. Psalm 37:7a says, "Rest in the Lord, and wait patiently for Him."

If you are praying for a godly husband of promise, it will require you to rest in the Lord as you patiently wait. The word *rest* can be defined as abide, trust, or remain steadfast. This can be difficult, especially if you have an ambitious personality trait. I fall into this category as my mind-set is "What needs to be done in order to make this happen?" If I have a goal, my thought process is to strategize a plan and take practical steps to meet that goal.

In my earlier years, I would tell God this is the time frame as to when I should meet my husband, followed by the time of year when we should get married. My motto was "Let's make a deal, Lord! I'll give You more prayer time and daily devotions if You bring me my godly husband of promise. I'll do this if You do that." That shows you how immature I was in my faith and my trust in God was severely lacking. Nevertheless, the Lord revealed to me that this is not a business transaction and if He chooses to bless me or not with a godly husband, He will do as He pleases.

Shortly after, I made no more deals or date setting with God. The Lord wanted me to learn the importance of resting in Him as He would bring about the promise in His time. He doesn't need any of us telling Him how and when He should do it. It says in Ecclesiastes 3:1, "To everything there is a season, a time for every purpose under heaven." As God's daughters, He wants us to truly rest in Him and allow Him to bring the promise of a godly husband to pass. Resting means placing your complete trust in Him, keeping your hands out of it, and believing God when there is no indication or sign that the promised husband is on the way.

Remember we walk by faith and not by sight. It's all in God's timing and not our own. Many of you may have heard this statement: God exists outside of time. He doesn't measure time as we do.

But, beloved, do not forget this one thing, that with the
Lord one day is as a thousand years, and
a thousand years as one day.
—2 Peter 3:8

God is faithfully working behind the scenes to bring you your godly husband of promise. He is divinely orchestrating both of your steps so the two of you can meet at the appointed time. Do not become discouraged; God's timing is absolutely and unequivocally perfect. He knows the date, the time, and the place when and where you will meet. The most important thing we are to do is to rest in the Lord while waiting on Him to bring the promise to pass.

> The steps of a good man are ordered by the
> Lord, and He delights in his way.
> —Psalm 37:23

CHAPTER 5

PRAYING FOR THE PROMISE

PRAYER IS A VITAL tool that should be a priority in the life of every believer, but oftentimes it is neglected. As children of God, we can sometimes follow the status quo of our culture by striving to get things quickly without praying and seeking the will of God first. We tend to make things happen on our own, which leads to creating bigger problems in the process, then trying to fix it, and after everything else fails, we decide to pray.

Prayer should be held in the highest regard and always be our first priority. Jesus is a Man of prayer and we see that in the gospel accounts. Likewise, we should follow His example and have daily communion with Him through prayer and the reading of His Word. I love what the psalmist says in Psalm 55:17: "Evening and morning and at noon I will pray, and cry aloud, and He shall hear my voice." The psalmist was committing himself to constant and persistent prayer unto the Lord. He spoke to Him throughout the day, trusting and believing that God was listening and would answer his prayers according to His perfect will and timing. We should have the same desire to pray without ceasing, knowing that God's ear is inclined to our requests while expecting Him to answer our petitions in line with His perfect will for our lives. God is never late or early but always right on time.

As you are waiting on God's best choice, be faithful in praying for him and entrust your husband to the Lord. If He has made this promise to you, He will be faithful in bringing it to pass at the appointed time. You do not need to try online dating or any other social networks to find a man. Trust me. I tried and failed, as I mentioned earlier. God knows you and your future husband. He has your addresses. You both are precious in His eyes. And He's working behind the scenes to bring you two together at the right time. The Lord has the master plan. His plan is far better than anything you and I can accomplish on our own. I encourage you ladies to continue to pray for your godly husbands of promise. Philippians 4:6 says, "Be anxious for nothing, but in everything by prayer and supplication, with thanksgiving, let your requests be made known to God."

While you are praying for the promise, keep busy at doing God's will for your life. Don't consume yourself in just praying for your godly husband. Ask God to impart His wisdom to you on how you should fulfill His purpose for your life. Everyone has a special calling on their lives. Actively seek God through prayer and His Word on how your life may bring glory and honor to His holy name. The Lord not only has a calling for you to be a wife but to be the godly woman who is faithful in doing His kingdom work.

In Luke 19:12–13, Jesus speaks a parable about a certain nobleman who went into a far country to receive for himself a kingdom and to return. So he called ten of his servants, delivered to them ten minas, and said to them, "Do business till I come." In the same sense, Jesus is effectively telling you and me to do work for His kingdom until He comes back. Walk worthy of your calling, remain faithful and diligent in doing His will, stay committed, and stay on the right course. We will all give an account for our lives when we stand before Him.

With that being said, please keep things in their proper perspective. First things first. Please be faithful in praying for

God's purpose to be fulfilled in your life. And secondly, pray for your godly husband of promise.

> But seek first the kingdom of God and His righteousness,
> and all these things shall be added to you.
> —Matthew 6:33

CHAPTER 6

PREPARING YOURSELF AS YOU WAIT

PREPARATION PLAYS A KEY role in most life events. Whether you are buying or renovating a home, planning a wedding, or going on vacation, all these things will include preparation. In the same sense, it's just as important to prepare yourself for your future godly husband of promise as you wait. Some may ask, "How do you do that?" Well, I would like to offer a few helpful hints that have been very beneficial in my season of waiting.

Begin by reading biblical books on how to be a godly wife and what is the role of the godly wife. There are so many great books out there. I advise that you ask your church or local Christian bookstore for recommendations.

If your church has a marriage ministry providing Bible study or workshop sessions, contact the coordinator and ask if you can sit in. This can be intimidating, but keep in mind your desire is to be a godly wife, and preparing yourself ahead of time will be better than trying to learn when you are already married. Personally, I participated in a handful of marriage workshop sessions. It was a little awkward to be the only single person among all married couples, but I couldn't allow fear or other uncomfortable feelings to sink in and keep me from being a part of those enriching sessions. In those settings, I was able to meet married couples, listen to great teaching, learn what my role is as a future godly wife, and participate in group discussions. The workshop sessions were a real blessing, which offered spiritual tools that will aid me in my desire to become a godly wife. If your church fellowship does not have a marriage ministry, get in touch with a Christian bookstore and ask for biblical CDs/DVDs on the different roles of a husband and wife in a godly marriage.

Additionally, start praying for your godly husband of promise and marriage. These essentials have been incorporated into my daily prayers. I went out and purchased a prayer journal specifically for my future godly husband. In it, I have written down prayers concerning his role as a godly husband (for him to love me as Christ loves the church). This also includes his calling (for him to always be obedient to the Lord, not to compromise his faith, and to fulfill the ministry God has called him to), his role as a godly father to our future children, God willing (to love and care for them, to encourage and build them up, and to not play favorites while we raise our kids together in the ways of the Lord), and his career (for him to always do his work unto the Lord).

Above are just examples to guide you in the preparation process as you are awaiting your godly husband of promise. Other factors can include learning how to cook or maybe becoming an outdoors person. A couple of years ago, I decided to take up different recreational hobbies, such as hiking and whale watching, just in case my future husband is an avid hiker or sea lover. With this in mind, I decided to challenge myself and go on a hiking expedition. Little did I know that it can be a real workout, especially if you are a first timer like myself. It was an experience which I will never forget.

Due to my lack of knowledge in hiking, I was unaware of the different ranges and levels of elevation.

The hike took place in the spring on a mild, cold evening

in Los Angeles. It was scheduled for two hours with a goal to reach elevations of roughly 1,600 feet. Upon my arrival, I was greeted by hiking guides who were leading the expedition. After cordial greetings were exchanged, I was given a waiver to sign in case anything happened—they would not be responsible. Further instructions were given of what trails we would be taking and what to expect during the hike. Listening to those directions should have been my first inclination to leave and not go on that adventure. Needless to say, I mustered up the courage to stay, said a quick prayer, and went on my hike.

Minutes into the hike, I was out of breath and calling myself an idiot for making this attempt. This hike was no joke, and it was definitely geared toward a more advanced and experienced person. The paths were narrow, followed by steep inclines and high elevations. I thought I was going to meet my Maker that night. But *praise* God, it started raining an hour into the hike. I couldn't have been happier. I was rejoicing. Due to the weather conditions, the hike was called off. Praise God!

I was really foolish to put myself in such a dangerous position. But thank God that even in the midst of my unwise decision, He was faithful to deliver me out of that situation. There is nothing wrong with hiking. I just made a poor judgment call to go on a more advanced expedition, which I was not equipped for. After that experience, I prayed to the Lord and said, "Maybe it's not a good idea to send me a man who likes to hike. Whale watching and sailing seem like less of a workout."

On a more serious note, please seek God's wisdom from His Word on how to be the godly wife He desires you to be. Preparation takes time and real commitment. It's not easy, but I encourage you to pray without ceasing and seek the Lord diligently in asking for His strength as He prepares you for this high calling. If God has spoken and promised you the blessing of a godly husband, He will definitely bring it to pass in His time and in His way. Don't lose heart!

Who can find a virtuous wife? For her worth is
far above rubies. The heart of her husband safely
trusts her; so he will have no lack of gain. She does
him good and not evil all the days of her life.
—Proverbs 31:10–12

In My Father's house are many mansions; if it were not so, I
would have told you. I go to prepare a place for you. And if I
go and prepare a place for you, I will come again and receive
you to Myself; that where I am, there you may be also.
—John 14:2–3

BELIEVING GOD WHEN YOU CAN'T SEE THE BIG PICTURE

WE'VE ALL HAD MOMENTS in our lives when we took steps of faith not knowing what the end results would be. There was a particular season in my life where I had to make a difficult decision concerning my late father's health and quality of life. In the interim, I had been praying for my dad's salvation off and on for a period of two years (2008–2010). At the beginning of 2010, the Lord had laid on my heart to start praying for my father's salvation more fervently. Prayers were lifted up daily on his behalf, and on occasion, I would witness to him when the opportunity presented itself.

During that time, my dad started experiencing extreme health issues that resulted in hospitalization and weeks of physical therapy. Long-term care was recommended for my father. Options included in-home care or a facility-based environment. Of course, none of this went well with my dad being the strong-willed man that he was. It was a scary time for both of us. But in my heart, I knew instantaneously it was what the Lord wanted and it was the best thing for my dad. Without having knowledge of board and care facilities or nursing homes, I prayed earnestly and asked my sisters in Christ to join me in prayer for the next steps. It was a hard road ahead with him wanting to come home while I struggled with the notion of putting him in a long-term care facility that might mistreat him. However, the Lord gave me affirmation to entrust my dad and the situation to Him.

Through bittersweet tears, I released my father into the loving hands of the Lord, and He faithfully took care of him. In the midst of it all, God had a wonderful plan that was being unfolded for my dad's salvation. Daily prayer was being offered up on my dad's behalf by one of my good friends and her husband. Over time, the Lord began softening my dad's heart, which resulted in him having a pleasant attitude and accepting things as they were. Things began to radically change for the best, beginning with our relationship as father and daughter. He stopped blaming me for his long-term care services. But the most important and life-changing event which took place was that my father gave his life to Christ when the gospel was shared with him. Praise the Lord! All the glory goes to our faithful King and High Priest! He orchestrates all of our life circumstances for our good, and there is nothing too difficult for the Lord.

> For with God nothing will be impossible.
> —Luke 1:37

During the times we're being tested, we can never see the big picture from the beginning, but we can trust that the Lord does. He knows the future and He holds our lives in His hands. He just requires us to take bold steps of faith and lean on Him throughout the whole process. Second Corinthians 5:7 tells us to walk by faith and not by sight. I didn't know the outcome in my father's situation from the beginning, but the Lord did. He taught me a valuable lesson in that season of my life, which continues to help me to this very day. When faced with any type of adversity, I need to run to the Lord first, entrust the situation to Him through prayer, and rely on Him to carry me through those dark valleys.

When you pass through the waters, I will be with
you; and through the rivers, they shall not overflow
you. When you walk through the fire, you shall
not be burned, nor shall the flame scorch you.
—Isaiah 43:2

Storms are not fun, and the majority of the time, we don't welcome them. But when the Lord sends them our way, He promises to be with us. He will never leave us nor forsake us (Hebrews 13:5b). In our trials, we all have a choice to either respond the correct way or not. Remember obedience is followed by the Lord's blessings. In my case, I had the opportunity to witness my father's conversion and see his life transformed into a new creation in Christ. And now he is safely home in the Savior's arms, and I will see him again on that faithful day.

If the Lord has promised you a godly husband, take Him at His word and believe He will bring the promise to pass, even though you can't see the big picture. God is working behind the scenes on your behalf.

God calls us to wait patiently on Him in faith. As I mentioned in an earlier chapter, never move ahead of God and think you will succeed in doing so. I'm sorry to say, but you will fail each time. Allow the Lord to lead you. I encourage you to wait on the Lord and believe and trust in Him for His best choice in a godly husband. The Lord will be faithful in bringing you two together at the appointed time. All self-efforts will only result in unnecessary heartache, anxiety, and frustration. The Lord doesn't need our help. He is Sovereign and in control of all our life events.

As daughters of the Most High King, we need to be godly women who exercise our faith and believe the promises God has spoken over our lives while trusting, abiding, and leaning on Him when we can't see the big picture. The Lord will always deliver on His Word. It will never return void.

Trust in the Lord with all your heart, and lean
not on your own understanding; in all your ways
acknowledge Him, and He shall direct your paths.
—Proverbs 3:5–6

The Lord of hosts has sworn, saying, "Surely,
as I have thought, so it shall come to pass, and
as I have purposed, so it shall stand.
—Isaiah 14:24

And the apostles said to the Lord, "Increase our faith."
—Luke 17:5

CHAPTER **8**

HAVING A GODLY AND MATURE WOMAN AS A MENTOR

I BELIEVE GOD PLACES CERTAIN people in our lives to pray for and encourage us in our walks with Christ. Years ago when I rededicated my life to the Lord, I was in need of spiritual guidance. My knowledge of what it meant to be filled with the Holy Spirit, how to pray, how to read my Bible, or what it meant to be a godly woman was unclear. So the Lord faithfully stepped in and brought me a godly woman to show me how to apply these spiritual truths/essentials to my walk with Him. She came alongside me and modeled the characteristics of how a godly woman should reflect the heart of Jesus. My friend was very instrumental in my life as she helped me to understand what it meant to maintain and cultivate my own personal relationship with the Lord.

As a woman who is waiting for your godly husband, it's very important to pray and ask the Lord to send you a god-fearing, believing woman as a mentor who will speak the truth of God's Word and model for you what it means to be a godly wife. Prayerfully consider this person. In addition, ask the Lord for wisdom on what type of setting will be best for you. The environment may either be one-on-one sessions with your mentor or group directed with other women seeking spiritual guidance on how to be a godly wife too. Whichever setting the Lord lays on your heart, continually ask the Lord to send you a strong believer who will give you counsel from God's Word on what it means to be a godly wife and not someone who will tell you what you want to hear.

We need biblical truth, ladies. Having a godly mentor does not substitute your reading of the Bible and your relationship with the Lord. Remember your mentor is not the Holy Spirit. You must remain anchored in the Lord and in His Word while seeking Him for biblical guidance. Your mentor is a vessel that God is using to help you gain biblical knowledge on what it means to be a godly wife as she shares her life experiences with you. She is not to be idolized or a crutch who you can lean on. Lean on the Lord and depend on Him always, for He is enough.

Godly mentors play a positive role in the lives of their mentees as they offer godly encouragement. In the book of 1 Timothy, we see how Paul (a seasoned believer) encouraged a young Timothy in his faith. In 1 Timothy 1:4, Paul urges Timothy not to give heed to fables and endless genealogies that causes disputes rather than godly edification, which is in faith. Again in 1 Timothy 6:12, he exhorts Timothy to fight the good fight of faith, to hold tightly to the eternal life to which God had called him, which he had declared so well before many witnesses. Just as Paul exhorted Timothy in his walk with Christ, you should have a godly and mature believing woman who will encourage you on your quest to be the godly wife that the Lord is calling you to be for His glory.

Staying anchored in God's Word and maintaining well-balanced fellowship with your mentor is very important. Work out a flexible schedule keeping her in mind. She may be widowed or a married woman with family priorities and other responsibilities. Please be cognizant and considerate of her time. Philippians 2:4

says, "Let each of you look out not only for his own interests, but also for the interests of others."

Make the most of your time with her. Be attentive to what your mentor is saying as she shares from her heart. Give her your undivided attention and politely listen to her without interjecting. If you have comments or questions, wait until she is done speaking. Keep a small notebook handy and ask your mentor, "Will it be okay to jot down verses and helpful details you share with me?" Ladies, if your mentor decides to share her life experiences with you, please be respectful and don't allow that information to go outside the walls of your conversation. Do not repeat what she said to other people or post it on your social media accounts. She is entrusting those details to you only. If your mentor decides to share with people you may know, let it come from her own mouth. Do not violate her trust. Relaying information to others can easily be turned into gossip with the truth being twisted. In Psalm 15:1–3 (NLT), the psalmist asks the Lord,

> Who may worship in your sanctuary, Lord? Who may enter your presence on your holy hill? Those who lead blameless lives and do what is right, speaking the truth from sincere hearts. Those who refuse to gossip or harm their neighbors or speak evil of their friends.

Proverbs 16:28 (NLT) says, "A troublemaker plants seeds of strife; gossip separates the best of friends." So ladies, I encourage you to keep what's shared between you and your mentor private and not repeat it.

Referring back to my earlier exhortation, please pray and ask the Lord to send you a female mentor. Keep in mind this should be a woman and not a man. In order to prevent the wrong relationships from forming or the development of feelings for a man who is not called to be your husband, it's best for women to be counseled by other women.

Follow the example of the apostle Paul as he encouraged Timothy in the faith. Notice that he was an older man encouraging a younger man in his walk with the Lord. Women should be counseled by other women and men should be counseled by men. There are certain situations when a pastor may counsel a woman when the individual is seeking pastoral guidance and/or direction and that's perfectly fine, as long as it's done in the appropriate setting. But in this special mentor/mentee relationship, it's wise to have an older woman as your mentor. Remember she should be a mature and strong believer, filled with the Holy Spirit while bearing the traits of a teachable spirit. Begin praying and asking the Lord for His wisdom and discernment on His divine choice in a godly woman as a mentor.

The older women likewise, that they be reverent in behavior, not slanderers, not given to much wine, teachers of good things—that they admonish the young women to love their husbands, to love their children, to be discreet, chaste, homemakers, good, obedient to their own husbands, that the word of God may not be blasphemed.
—Titus 2:3–5

CHAPTER 9

REMAINING IN GODLY FELLOWSHIP

WE'VE OFTEN HEARD THE phrase "Birds of a feather flock together" or "Show me your friends, and I'll show you who you are." We are all identified by the company we keep. It's imperative to choose your friends wisely and spend quality time with other mature godly believers. The Bible affirms in Proverbs 12:26, "The righteous should choose his friends carefully, for the way of the wicked leads them astray."

Let me paint a scenario for you. You are patiently waiting on the Lord to bring you His best. And maybe you have a girlfriend who is also a believer; however, she is compromised in that area of her life on waiting for a godly husband. Possibly she has settled for second best and is currently dating a nice guy who is a nonbeliever with a plan to convert him. You and I know that this is definitely in no way, shape, or form God's plan. His desire is to give you His absolute best—a God-fearing, believing man who knows and loves the Lord above everyone and everything else while keeping Him first in all areas of his life. Anything less than this is a lie from the devil.

Ladies, don't settle because you feel that you are getting older or your biological clock is ticking. Whether you are in your mature teens, twenties, thirties, forties, fifties, sixties, seventies, eighties, or beyond, if God has promised you a godly husband, He will be faithful in bringing the promise to pass. He is God and with Him nothing is impossible. He delivered on His promise to Abraham and Sarah when He blessed them with their son, Isaac. If Sarah can have a baby at ninety, certainly God is more than able to bring you His best choice in a godly husband. I don't know about you, but I'm believing God for great things.

> Now to Him who is able to do exceedingly
> abundantly above all that we ask or think,
> according to the power that works in us.
> —Ephesians 3:20

With this being said, ladies, it's extremely important for you to spend quality time with other like-minded sisters in Christ who will encourage and pray for you as you wait patiently for God's best. Keeping close fellowship with a compromised believer is a downward spiral to you learning their ways, which will lead to you drifting away from the path that God has for you. I'm not saying to reject your friend. Instead, Galatians 6:1b exhorts us, "You who are spiritual restore such a one in a spirit of gentleness, considering yourself lest you also be tempted." Pray for her, and encourage her that she will get back on the right path. In the same token, you need to exercise wisdom in spending time with this person if she is living in sin. You may need to distance yourself from the individual for a while until she repents, turns away from that lifestyle, and restores her relationship with the Lord.

> Do you not know that a little leaven
> leavens the whole lump?
> —1 Corinthians 5:6b

I have a host of sisters in Christ who are very dear to my

heart. We pray and encourage each other in the Lord. We enjoy fellowship with one another over lunch and coffee, in Bible study, and in other church-related events. What I admire most about my sisters in Christ is that I see the light and love of Jesus in every single one of them. It is shown in their words and actions and in their own unique ways. They seek first to honor and praise the Lord for what He's doing in their individual lives. Their desire is to maintain a strong close walk with Him and do His will while allowing the Lord to use them for His glory. Witnessing their godly behavior stirs up a much deeper thirst for the Lord and His Word within my own life and inspires me to continue to run my race well for my Savior, keeping my eyes firmly fixed on Him.

As iron sharpens iron, so a friend sharpens a friend.
—Proverbs 27:17 (NLT)

Ladies, I can't stress how vital it is to remain in godly fellowship with like-minded believers. Our friends have a major influence on our lives. Please make it a high priority to spend quality time with sisters in Christ who will build you up in your faith, pray for you, and encourage you in your walk with the Lord as you are waiting on the Lord for His best choice in a godly husband.

Do not be deceived: "Evil company corrupts good habits."
-1 Corinthians 15:33

CHAPTER 10

SAVING AND KEEPING
YOURSELF PURE

IN OUR CULTURE TODAY, sex is a popular trend among teenagers, young adults, and unmarried couples. Sexual immorality has become the social norm with people living together before marriage and married couples being unfaithful to their spouses. The Bible clearly points out that sex is reserved and blessed by God in a marital relationship between a man and his wife.

> Marriage is honorable among all, and the bed undefiled;
> but fornicators and adulterers God will judge.
> —Hebrews 13:4

Sex is not a sin. It becomes a sin when it is used in a way to dishonor God. God created sex, which is to be enjoyed between a husband and wife within the boundaries of a marital covenant. Ladies, I encourage you to begin saving and keeping yourself pure for your godly husband of promise. Do not engage in any type of sexual activity until you are married. First Corinthians 6:19–20 (NLT) says,

> Don't you realize that your body is the temple of the Holy
> Spirit, who lives in you and was given to you by God?

You do not belong to yourself, for God bought you with a high price. So you must honor God with your body.

Therefore, you should honor God with your vessels (bodies) and abstain from all types of premarital sex. Don't put yourself in a position where you can fall in this area.

Aside from the physical aspect, I will like to encourage you ladies to not give your hearts and emotions away. Personally, I don't believe in keeping close friendships with the opposite sex. It can be detrimental, and you might find yourself developing feelings for someone who you're not called to marry. Or my future godly husband might see me out with a male friend and get the wrong idea. I want to reserve my heart and my emotions for my husband only.

In our courting relationship and marriage, my prayer for my husband and me is not to have or maintain close relationships with friends of the opposite sex. It just creates problems and can possibly be an open door to an emotional connection with the individual in question or an adulterous relationship. I believe in safeguarding my marriage and not giving the enemy a foothold to come in to destroy it. Every marriage will be tested and have its share of problems. It's inevitable. But I believe in putting up parameters to protect my future marriage, and it goes along with neither my husband nor me having these types of relationships. The devil is very cunning and will do anything to destroy God's marital design between a man and a woman. Mark 10:9 says, "Therefore what God has joined together, let not man separate."

During this time of waiting, some of you may be inclined to go out and casually date due to loneliness or a need for companionship. It's tough. Believe me. I know. But I must say that doing so will only lead to heartache, disappointment, and the possibility of you developing feelings and marrying the wrong person. Don't expose your heart and emotions to be used and abused; instead, keep them reserved for your godly husband of promise to be cherished by him. Prayerfully ask the Lord to infuse you with His strength and enabling to wait and not date. The exhortation in Philippians 4:13 says, "I can do all things through Christ who strengthens me."

Be a virtuous woman and choose the high road; honor the Lord with your body and heart. It will indeed be challenging, but as you rely and depend solely on the Lord and His strength, He will enable you to keep yourself pure physically and emotionally while waiting on His best choice for your life. It takes self-discipline as you condition your mind and thoughts to be completely focused on the things of the Lord rather than the things of the world. Don't give any opportunities for the flesh. Paul says in Galatians 5:16, "I say then: Walk in the Spirit, and you shall not fulfill the lust of the flesh."

Another exhortation is found in John 6:63, where Jesus says, "It is the Spirit who gives life; the flesh profits nothing. The words that I speak to you are spirit, and they are life." Second Corinthians 10:5b says to bring every thought into captivity to the obedience of Christ.

My prayer is that these verses will resonate in your heart and give you a fresh outlook on God's perspective. These are pearls of wisdom that the Lord has shared with me, and my prayer is that you will take hold of them and live out these standards as His daughter who is patiently waiting on the godly husband of promise from her Savior.

Finally, brethren, whatever things are true, whatever
things are noble, whatever things are just, whatever things
are pure, whatever things are lovely, whatever things
are of good report, if there is any virtue and if there is
anything praiseworthy-meditate on these things.
—Philippians 4:8

Ladies, please honor the Lord with your body and place a

protective guard around your heart. Remain pure physically as well as emotionally, and ask God to continually strengthen you in saving yourself completely until you are married to His divine choice in a godly husband.

CHAPTER 11

NOT BEING LED BY
YOUR EMOTIONS

SOMETIMES AS WOMEN, WE tend to allow our feelings and emotions to drive the way we think and react, and then we allow them to make our final decisions in any given situation. Personally, I've had far too many predicaments where I relied on my emotions instead of God's Word.

A while back, I was involved in a relationship and the ending of it nearly crushed me; however, it led to my rededication back to Christ. As I began my journey of walking with the Lord, this person was still in my heart at the time, and I yearned for the Lord to save him and restore our relationship. I began praying for his salvation with the hopes that the Lord will fulfill these wishes.

This went on for a couple of years, but the Lord was giving me confirmation through prayer and circumstances that the answer was no. This individual was not God's best for me. I wish I could tell you that I heeded God's voice during that season of my life, but I didn't. Instead, I gave full control over to my emotions and feelings and allowed them to govern my thoughts into believing that this person was my godly husband of promise. I couldn't have been further from the truth.

Due to my stubbornness and willful disobedience, I sank into a deep depression and began having suicidal thoughts. This was an extremely hard time in my life. Some days I would be okay, and other days were filled with uncontrollable tears. It was very difficult to have my quiet time with the Lord. Literally, I had to force myself to read my Bible while trying to hold back tears because I was so discouraged. But what I realized was the more I immersed myself in God's Word, the Lord began to mend my broken heart while lifting that heavy burden off my shoulders. Finally, I was able to accept His answer of no.

So ladies, when God says no, quickly accept His answer while trusting and believing it's His way of protecting you. He sees something farther down the road which will potentially harm you and eventually hinder your relationship with Him. Remember the Lord sees the big picture and knows what's best for you. God loves you so much and doesn't want to see you get hurt. When He says no to the wrong person, don't lose heart. Be grateful. The Lord knows a relationship with the wrong man will destroy you mentally, emotionally, and in some cases, physically. Instead, give thanks to God for closing the doors. Begin praising Him that His divine choice in the promised husband is on the way.

As you are waiting on the Lord to bring you your godly husband of promise, beware of wolves in sheep's clothing or counterfeits. We have an adversary, the devil, who walks about like a roaring lion seeking whom he may devour. He will do anything and everything to deter you from having God's best. The enemy is very deceptive in all his schemes, and if you are not anchored in God's Word and in your relationship with Him, you will fall prey to his tactics. He watches and studies you to see what your vulnerabilities are in order to use them against you. He may bring you someone who may seem as though he is the godly husband of promise, but in fact, it's a beautifully wrapped counterfeit package from the enemy. Ladies, you cannot allow yourself to be led by your emotions and feelings. Instead, continually ask the Lord to give you spiritual discernment and wisdom so you can discern the truth from a lie. It's so important for you to seek the Lord in His wisdom and allow His Holy Spirit to guide you in all areas of your life, not just in your wait for a godly husband.

> If any of you lacks wisdom, let him ask of God,
> who gives to all liberally and without
> reproach, and it will be given to him.
> —James 1:5

> Wisdom is the principal thing; therefore get wisdom. And
> in all your getting, get understanding. Exalt her, and she
> will promote you; she will bring you honor, when you
> embrace her. She will place on your head an ornament
> of grace; a crown of glory she will deliver to you.
> —Proverbs 4:7–9

Let these verses permeate your heart as you are waiting on the gift of a godly husband. Ladies, please don't allow your emotions to lead you, but allow the Holy Spirit of God to lead, direct, and guide you on His good, perfect, and righteous path.

> Show me Your ways, O Lord; teach me Your paths.
> Lead me in Your truth and teach me, for You are the
> God of my salvation; on You I wait all the day.
> —Psalm 25:4–5

> He restores my soul; He leads me in the paths
> of righteousness for His name's sake.
> —Psalm 23:3

CHAPTER **12**

THANKING GOD FOR
THE PROMISE

THANKFULNESS IS ANOTHER FORM of praise God calls us to exercise as believers. Ephesians 5:20 says, "To give thanks always for all things to God the Father in the name of our Lord Jesus Christ." We should always thank and praise God for who He is and rejoice in Him, because He is worthy of all our praise. We should thank Him for our relationships to Him, for His faithfulness in our lives, for all of His provisions, for answered prayers, for our trials (in them we see His hand at work, which turns out for His glorification followed by our faith being strengthened in Him), and for the blessing of family and friends. Thankfulness should be at the heart of every believer. It should be ingrained in our thoughts and minds. First Thessalonians 5:18 exhorts us by stating, "In everything give thanks; for this is the will of God in Christ Jesus for you."

As daughters belonging to Christ, we need to begin thanking and praising Him for our godly husbands of promise. Start rejoicing in Him that the promise is on the way. Verbalize your gratitude to God through continued prayer and scriptural reading. Go to Him and express,

Lord, I believe and trust that You will bring me Your best choice in a godly husband in Your own way and time. I praise You in advance for directing our steps toward each other. I will stand on Your promise Lord trusting that You will bring it to pass. I will rest fully and completely in You while knowing that the answer is on the way. You alone are worthy, Lord! Thank You for handpicking Your very best for me.

> Let us come before His presence with
> thanksgiving; let us shout joyfully
> to Him with psalms.
> —Psalm 95:2

> Enter into His gates with thanksgiving,
> and into His courts with praise. Be thankful
> to Him, and bless His name.
> —Psalm 100:4

Also, begin thanking the Lord in advance for His blessing and anointing on the beginning of a lasting godly friendship, courtship, relationship, and marriage with your future husband in which it will always bring glory, honor, and praise to His holy name. Pray and ask God to mold you two into the image of His Son, Jesus, in order that you both will become more like Him and be joined together as one flesh. Thankfulness is very important in the eyes of God, and it pleases His heart when we reverence Him in this way.

> I will praise the name of God with a song,
> and will magnify Him with thanksgiving.
> —Psalm 69:30

EPILOGUE

My dearest sisters in Christ, I hope and pray that this book has ministered to your hearts and has encouraged you to rest in the Lord and wait patiently on Him for His best choice in a godly husband of promise. We may not understand the reasons for the delay, but we must continue to trust in God and stand on His unchanging word that He is faithful to deliver on all of His promises in His own way and time. We serve a mighty God who is majestic in all of His ways, and He is able to do exceedingly, abundantly, and above all we ask or think. My heart rejoices because I know that God will answer our prayers according to His perfect will for each of our lives. I'm looking forward to hearing the many testimonies of how the Lord has strategically worked in your lives to bring about the promised husband as well as seeing the fruit of your answered prayers.

> My God, my God, how awesome You are! You are the King of kings and the Lord of lords. You are the One and true living God, and there is none other but You. I offer up praise, honor, and thanksgiving to You for all the ladies who have read this book, including myself. Lord, my prayer is that You will give us hearts to faithfully love You first and foremost as our Heavenly Husband, to keep You as our first love, to faithfully love You more than we love our earthly husbands.

> God, You come first in our lives. Please give us Your wisdom, strength, and power to keep and love You ten thousand times more than we love our godly husbands of

promise. Although a priceless gift from You, help us not to idolize or put our husbands before You. You said in Your Word that You are a jealous God and You will not tolerate one's affection for any other gods. So Lord, help us not to esteem our husbands as idols. You are number 1, and I pray that our personal relationships with You will grow stronger and deeper as we seek to please You as godly women and future godly wives.

Lord, I pray for You to give us a stronger desire to wait patiently on You for our godly husbands of promise. As we wait, Lord, I pray we will be about our Father's business fulfilling the calls You have placed on our lives. Also, I pray that we will seek You diligently in living out the purposes You intended for us individually.

Lord, please give us Your wisdom on what all that entails and empower us with Your Holy Spirit to live out our God-given assignments while fulfilling Your perfect will to further Your kingdom on this earth. Lord, thank You that You have Your very best for each of us, and I praise You with a grateful heart.

I thank You that our godly husbands of promise are on the way. When You bring each of us Your divine choice, Lord, please give us Your godly wisdom to know it's the godly man You have appointed. My prayer is that it will be the beginning of an anointed, blessed, and lasting godly friendship, courtship, relationship, and marriage that will always bring glory and honor to Your holy name.

Heavenly Father, I lift up this prayer request to You in humility, in faith, in thanksgiving, and in praise. I ask that You answer it

according to Your perfect will for our lives. In Your Son Jesus'
name, I pray. Amen.

> Wait on the Lord; be of good courage, and He shall
> strengthen your heart; wait, I say, on the Lord!
> —Psalm 27:14

> No good thing will He withhold from
> those who walk uprightly.
> —Psalm 84:11b

Printed in the United States
By Bookmasters